Original title:
Rising Whispers Under the Elf Frame

Copyright © 2025 Swan Charm

Author: Kaido Väinamäe
ISBN HARDBACK: 978-1-80559-351-5
ISBN PAPERBACK: 978-1-80559-850-3

Scents of Magic In the Twilight

The evening whispers soft and sweet,
With hints of jasmine in the air.
A breeze that dances, light on feet,
Brings secrets wrapped in twilight's care.

Stars blink like candles, oh so bright,
As shadows waltz upon the ground.
In every corner, pure delight,
The world wraps dreams in love profound.

Moonlight drapes the earth in silver,
Painting paths of dreams and sighs.
In stillness, nature starts to quiver,
As hearts unite 'neath starlit skies.

Scent of pine and dew-kissed rose,
Mingle as night begins to breathe.
Magic stirs where beauty flows,
In quiet moments, we believe.

So linger long in twilight's gaze,
Embrace the calm that twilight brings.
For in these hours, the heart sways,
And whispers softly, as it sings.

Echoes of the Heart Beneath the Tall Trees

Underneath the towering boughs,
Where sunlight peeks through leafy veils,
The heart finds peace as nature bows,
In whispered winds and playful trails.

Leaves rustle tales of long-lost dreams,
Each echo holds a story bright.
As shadows dance, the sunlight beams,
In secret spaces, hearts take flight.

Mossy carpets soften our way,
While gentle streams sing songs of ease.
In nature's arms, we long to stay,
Among the giants, spirits tease.

Every sigh from ancient wood,
Speaks wisdom deep as roots go down.
In tranquil thoughts, we feel what's good,
Beneath the trees, we shed our crown.

So gather close, where echoes dwell,
Let laughter ripple through the leaves.
In moments shared, our hearts do swell,
Beneath the tall trees, magic weaves.

The Soil of Silent Secrets

Beneath the ground, whispers lie,
Roots entwined, hopes gone awry.
In the dark, stories sleep,
Silent secrets, ours to keep.

A gentle breeze stirs the leaves,
Nature's tongue, it softly weaves.
In every petal, a tale told,
In every grain, a dream behold.

The soil cradles what we yearn,
In its embrace, we shall learn.
Mysterious past, shadows blend,
Forgotten paths that never end.

Crimson blooms on emerald beds,
Life emerges, where spirit treads.
From hidden depths, a world extends,
In every heart, the soil mends.

Underneath the fading light,
Seeds of hope grow, taking flight.
In the silence, let us find,
The soil holds what's left behind.

Flickers of Grace in the Forest

Golden rays through branches peek,
Dancing softly, nature's speak.
In the stillness, hearts align,
Flickers of grace, a sacred sign.

Whispers echo among the pines,
Tales of old in gentle lines.
Mossy carpets and shadows play,
Grace unfolds in a serene ballet.

Crisp air wraps the wandering soul,
Nature's beauty makes us whole.
Each step taken, a prayer sent,
Among the trees, time is spent.

Birdsong threads through the tree's weave,
A melody that makes us believe.
In every flutter, truth imbues,
Flickers of grace, we can't refuse.

As twilight calls with its soft glide,
Mysteries in the dark reside.
With every whisper, love's embrace,
We find our peace in the forest's grace.

Celestial Shadows and Dappled Light

Between the stars, a soft sigh flows,
Where celestial secrets gently pose.
In twilight's glow, shadows blend,
A world where dreams and wonders send.

Dappled light on the river's stream,
Whispers of night weave a soft dream.
In silver beams, a dance takes flight,
Celestial shadows embrace the night.

Moonlit pathways call to the lost,
Navigating by hope, not the cost.
With every turn, the heart ignites,
In the dark, are found the lights.

Constellations paint the sky high,
Stories told from bright to shy.
Among the cosmic tapestry spun,
Celestial whispers remind us we're one.

The universe in each heartbeat glows,
In shadows and light, love ever grows.
Together we wander, hand in hand,
In celestial realms, we forever stand.

Guideposts from Elven Hearts

Through ancient woods where echoes play,
Elven hearts light the way.
With gentle steps and wisdom's grace,
Guideposts stand in sacred space.

Misty trails weave through the glen,
Whispers of lore, again and again.
In the stillness, messages bloom,
Elven wisdom dispels the gloom.

With silver gleams upon the stream,
Their laughter floats like a sweet dream.
In every leaf, a truth imparts,
Marking paths from elven hearts.

When shadows creep and doubts arise,
The light from within ignites the skies.
In unity, they softly sing,
Guideposts shining in everything.

So when the night feels far too long,
Trust in the magic, where you belong.
For in the forest, let love start,
In every echo, an elven heart.

Secrets of the Sylvan Shadows

In the morning mist they dwell,
Whispers soft, a hidden spell.
Winds of change through leaves they weave,
Ancient tales they gently breathe.

Beneath the oak, a secret holds,
Life's embrace, the forest molds.
Step with care, the ground may sigh,
Echoes of days long gone by.

Mossy paths invite the brave,
To seek the warmth the shadows gave.
Creatures stir in twilight's glow,
Guarding truths we long to know.

Songs of silence fill the air,
A magic found, if you dare.
In the hollows, shadows blend,
Enchanted worlds around the bend.

When night descends, the secrets hum,
The heart of woods, a steady drum.
Embrace the quiet, let it flow,
For in the hush, the answers grow.

Echoes Beneath the Canopy

Softly spoken, whispers call,
Under branches, shadows fall.
Each rustling leaf, a sacred verse,
Nature's breath, a universe.

Misty trails where dreams may lead,
Stories hidden, hearts take heed.
In the dappled light we tread,
Paths less traveled, dreams unsaid.

Frosted mornings, twilight's grace,
Gentle breezes warm embrace.
Beneath the boughs, secrets twine,
Echoing through the sacred pine.

Stars peek down through leafy seams,
Awakening our deepest dreams.
Silence sings in twilight's hue,
Binding past with the present view.

As we wander, time stands still,
Nature's pulse, a lover's thrill.
In the whispers, hearts align,
Echoes faint, forever shine.

Enchanted Murmurs of Twilight

When day gives way to softened light,
Murmurs weave through the coming night.
Dusk unveils its magic glow,
Revealing worlds we long to know.

Petals close, the stars will blink,
Nature pauses, time to think.
In fragrant air, the scent of dreams,
Whispers flow like gentle streams.

Moonlit dances 'neath the trees,
Promises stirred by fragrant breeze.
Echoed laughter fills the glade,
In twilight's arms, all fears fade.

Secret pathways beckon near,
Guided softly by our fear.
Every shadow, a tale to tell,
In this hush, our souls rebel.

As night unfolds its velvet cloth,
Murmurs speak of sacred troth.
In silence deep, we find our way,
To dreams that linger, night or day.

The Luminous Path of Feylight

A shimmering trail, the feylight glows,
Where magic dances, time bestows.
Stepping lightly, hearts in flight,
On this path of pure delight.

Glistening trails through misty air,
Dreams awaken, enchantments flare.
Guided by the stars above,
Nature sings a song of love.

In the twilight's soft embrace,
Fairies whisper, leave no trace.
Footprints lost in silver dew,
As night reveals a world anew.

Luminous visions, soft and bright,
Awakening within the night.
Secrets spun in silken thread,
In the feylight, all are led.

So take my hand, let fears take flight,
Journey forth in feylight's sight.
Together woven, fate entwined,
On paths where magic souls aligned.

Echoing Lullabies of the Nightwood

In the woods where shadows play,
Whispers dance with moonlit sway.
Crickets hum a gentle tune,
Cradled by the silver moon.

Branches sway with tender grace,
Softly hiding time and space.
Nature sings her soothing song,
Lullabies the night prolong.

Breezes brush against the trees,
Carrying the night's soft pleas.
Echoes linger, sweet and clear,
Wrapping dreams that we hold dear.

Stars above in silence glow,
Guiding where the rivers flow.
Every creature blends in night,
Merging shadows, heart's delight.

As the dawn begins to creep,
In the night, our secrets keep.
Echoing through the nightwood's heart,
From the dreamers, never part.

Currents of Magic in the Air

In the twilight, colors weave,
Magic stirs in the mind to believe.
Whispers float on the evening breeze,
Carrying dreams like dancing leaves.

Mysterious sparks light the skies,
Where the horizon and daydreams rise.
Threads of fate entwined with stars,
Mapping journeys to distant bars.

Every sigh in the vibrant night,
Hints of wonders, visions bright.
As laughter mingles with the sighs,
Lost in the dance where enchantment lies.

From the shadows, spirits play,
Guiding hearts along the way.
Currents flow through whispered thoughts,
Leaving trails that time forgot.

Among the clouds, secrets swirl,
In the air, emotions twirl.
With each heartbeat, magic sings,
Filling dreams with timeless wings.

The Soft Glow of Mythic Hues

Underneath the starry dome,
Colors blend, a vibrant home.
Radiance spills through ancient trees,
Whispering tales carried on the breeze.

Golden light on emerald leaves,
Chasing shadows that darkness weaves.
Every hue a story spun,
In the twilight, we become one.

From the earth, a magic grows,
Illuminated by dusk's soft glows.
Painting memories on the air,
Crafted gently, beyond compare.

As the night stirs with delight,
Dreams awaken within the night.
Boundless shades of pure embrace,
In the glow, we find our place.

Softly laughing, time will bend,
Myths and legends never end.
In this realm of mystic views,
Every heart beats with vibrant hues.

Secrets Linger in the Leafy Embrace

In the forest's gentle hold,
Stories whispered, secrets told.
Leaves that shuffle, rustle near,
Carrying laughter, hope, and cheer.

Every branch a prison bare,
Holding dreams beyond compare.
Underneath the growing shade,
Ancient memories softly made.

Silent glimmers within the dusk,
Mingling scents of earth and musk.
In the shadows, mysteries lie,
Glimpses of worlds, unbound by sky.

Roots entangle in timeless dust,
Forging bonds of love and trust.
Among the ferns, peace unfurls,
Binding souls in nature's swirls.

As the day whispers goodbye,
Dreams awake beneath the sky.
In the leaves that softly sway,
Secrets linger where they play.

Currents of Magic in Tranquil Air

Whispers dance on gentle breeze,
Carrying secrets, soft and clear.
A flicker of light beneath the trees,
Nature's wonders held so dear.

Ripples in pools of glimmering night,
Stars reflect in waters deep.
A shimmering glow, a fleeting sight,
Awakens dreams while the world sleeps.

Swaying branches, stories untold,
Woven in shadows, secrets swell.
The heart of the forest, ancient and bold,
Holds memories where the wild things dwell.

With each breath, magic unfolds,
In tranquil air, a world sublime.
Echoes of laughter, soft and cold,
Caught in the rhythm, lost in time.

Here, in this stillness, we find our place,
Among the currents, emotions swirl.
Awash in beauty, we embrace
The woven threads of life's great whirl.

The Thread of Stars Through the Trees

Silver strands weave through the night,
Kisses of light on emerald leaves.
Each flicker shines with whispered delight,
A tapestry of dreams it weaves.

Branches cradle the cosmic scene,
Embracing the whispers of ancient lore.
Beneath the boughs, the veil is thin,
As starlit stories come to the fore.

In the moon's glow, shadows play,
Rustling softly, nature's choir.
The thread of stars leads the way,
A shimmering path of wonder and fire.

Glimmers of hope in each tiny spark,
Dancing gently, the night's sweet song.
Through the trees, 'til the dawn is stark,
We weave our tales, where we belong.

In this embrace of night's cool grace,
The stars remind us of love's embrace.

Veiled Stories Among the Leaves

Hidden tales in rustling sheets,
Whispers of life in colors fair.
Every leaf a secret greets,
Veiled stories float in fragrant air.

Through tangled vines, forgotten dreams,
Echoes of voices long since passed.
Nature's canvas, where hope redeems,
Each moment painted, forever cast.

Gentle breezes kiss the ground,
Awakening memories, old and wise.
Nature holds mysteries profound,
In every shadow, the past lies.

Cascading light through branches sway,
Illuminates whispers of time's embrace.
Among the leaves, where we play,
Veiled stories entwined in grace.

As seasons change, new tales arise,
In nature's heart, surrounded by bliss.

Enchanted Pathways in the Gloom

In twilight's grasp, the pathways wind,
Shadows deepen, secrets bloom.
Lost in a world where stars aligned,
The essence of magic fills the room.

Through tangled roots and whispers low,
Every step a tale retold.
On enchanted trails, where wonders flow,
The heart discovers treasures bold.

Mystic echoes guide the way,
Footprints linger in the mist.
In haunted glades, where shadows play,
The promise of adventure exists.

Twinkling lights lead us on,
In the gloom, hope gleams anew.
As the night fades into dawn,
We chase the dreams that linger true.

With every breath, the magic streams,
In enchanted pathways, we find our dreams.

Veiled Melodies of the Forest

In the hush of morning light,
Whispers dance on emerald boughs.
Softly sing the hidden songs,
Nature's voice, a gentle pause.

Mossy beds where secrets rest,
Carried lightly by the breeze.
Echoes weave through ancient trees,
Nestled deep in quiet pleas.

Sunlight filters, golden rays,
Touching leaves with tender grace.
Branches sway in rhythmic play,
Though no soul can see this space.

Deer tread softly on the ground,
Rabbits dart from shade to shade.
Life erupts without a sound,
In glens where dreams are made.

As twilight falls, the songs remain,
Melodies on night's soft breath.
A symphony of joy and pain,
In forests bound to hidden depth.

Glimmers of Forgotten Whispers

In shadows cast by time's embrace,
Echoes linger, yet unseen.
Whispers float through empty space,
Memories wrapped in silver sheen.

Old bricks bear the weight of tales,
Voices once bright now fade away.
Breezes carry haunting gales,
As sunlight dims at end of day.

Chasing phantoms of the past,
Glimmers spark in fading light.
In the silence, shadows cast,
Whispers beckon to the night.

Beneath the stars, a chorus sighs,
Each note a fragment of time lost.
Carried gently on night's sighs,
A melody, no matter the cost.

Yet in the dark, a promise glows,
With every night, the stories breathe.
Hidden truths the fabric sows,
Glimmers shine in those who believe.

The Touch of Celestial Leaves

Underneath the twilight sky,
Stars weave through the stretching night.
Whispered dreams in branches lie,
Leaves shimmer with a silver light.

Each leaf holds a story bright,
Of planets, comets, and the moon.
Nature's hand, a cosmic sight,
Cradles dreams in silent tunes.

The breeze carries tales untold,
Of galaxies that spin and swirl.
In the dark, the magic unfolds,
As time dances in a twirl.

Celestial whispers brush the air,
A symphony of night's embrace.
With every rustle, hearts laid bare,
The universe in nature's grace.

At dawn, the world begins to wake,
Yet twilight holds its quiet keep.
Each moment, new paths to take,
Under leaves where secrets seep.

The Language of Shadows at Dusk

When daylight fades and colors blend,
Shadows stretch, a quiet spell.
In dusky light, the spirits mend,
Silent whispers cast their shell.

Each figure tells a tale of yore,
Languages lost in time's deep flow.
Stories echo forevermore,
In the twilight's fleeting glow.

Figures dance upon the ground,
Mysteries wrapped in shades of grey.
Where silence speaks without a sound,
As light fades gently away.

The moon rises in regal grace,
Illuminating truths once masked.
In this transient, sacred space,
The world listens for what's asked.

As night unfolds, we hear the call,
Embrace the dusk, our hearts awake.
In shadows, we find truths for all,
A language born in dreams we make.

Flickers of Wonder in the Dim

In the twilight's gentle embrace,
Soft glimmers dance, whispers trace.
Worlds unfold in shadowed light,
Courage blooms, heart takes flight.

Each flicker a tale, a secret told,
Dreams ignited, stories bold.
Laughter echoes in the air,
Hope ignites, a sweet affair.

Through the dark, a path appears,
Guided softly by the years.
Twinkling stars, a guiding spark,
Leading souls through the dark.

With every heartbeat, magic flows,
Painting futures, where love grows.
In the dim, we find our way,
Embracing night, welcoming day.

Flickers of wonder, spirits rise,
In the quiet, we meet the skies.
In the heart of darkness, we see
The light within, wild and free.

The Harmony of Heartwood Dreams

Beneath the branches, shadows weave,
Songs of time no hearts believe.
Whirling whispers, breezes play,
Nature's pulse, forever sway.

In the timber's gentle core,
Lies a truth, a hidden door.
Each heartbeat echoes, soft and bright,
Guided by the inner light.

Woven deep in roots and earth,
Dreams awaken, dance of birth.
Harmony sings through leafy boughs,
Alive in silence, sacred vows.

Amongst the trees, together stand,
A living choir, hand in hand.
Every leaf a note of cheer,
Resonating, crystal clear.

In heartwood dreams, we find our place,
In the whispers, time and space.
Here in nature, love aligns,
As harmony forever shines.

Whispers of the Stardust Grove

In the hush of twilight's veil,
Stardust whispers, soft and frail.
Trees adorned in silver light,
Secrets held in velvet night.

Every branch a story spun,
Every glow, a race begun.
Stars above, watching close,
Cradling dreams, a gentle dose.

Through the grove, the shadows glide,
Lost in wonder, hearts abide.
Moonlit paths, forever chase,
Echoes of a timeless grace.

In the stillness, starlight streams,
Carving out our wildest dreams.
Every sigh a cosmic plea,
In this grove, we're wild and free.

Whispers linger, soft and low,
Guiding hearts where lovers go.
In the stardust, we will find,
A universe, forever kind.

Shadows that Speak of Ancient Lore

In the twilight's tender grasp,
Shadows weave a whispered clasp.
Tales of old, secrets unfold,
In their depths, histories told.

Figures dance in moonlit glow,
Echoing paths that we might know.
Ancient trees, their branches bend,
Guardians, timeless, they transcend.

Through the echoes, voices call,
Reciting legends that enthrall.
Secrets rustle in the breeze,
A chorus of soft memories.

In the dark, a fire's light,
Beneath the stars, we share the night.
Stories spun from ages past,
In the shadows, truths amassed.

Each whisper carries a refrain,
Binding heart and soul like chain.
Shadows dance, forevermore,
As they speak of ancient lore.

The Breath of Enchantment

In twilight's glow, a whisper stirs,
A dance of shadows, soft as fur.
Moonlight weaves through ancient trees,
The night unfolds, a gentle tease.

Petals sigh with fragrant dreams,
As stars align in silken streams.
Magic lingers in the air,
Awakening the heart's old care.

A breeze that speaks of hidden things,
The song of night on silken wings.
In every sound a tale is spun,
Creating worlds where dreams are won.

With every breath, a secret shared,
In this embrace, the soul lay bared.
Such splendor in the hour of rest,
Where every heartbeat feels its best.

The night, a cloak of soft delight,
In its warmth, we find our light.
The breath of enchantment beckons near,
Entwining hearts, erasing fear.

Nature's Rhapsody in Silence

Beneath the boughs, where shadows play,
A serenade of night and day.
The river hums its gentle song,
In nature's arms, we all belong.

Leaves whisper secrets to the stars,
Their stories told from near to far.
The mountains listen, wise and grand,
Their silence is a guiding hand.

In stillness lies a symphony,
A world at peace in harmony.
The call of owls, a sacred tune,
And crickets play beneath the moon.

With every rustle, life unfolds,
Tales of wonders, age-old and bold.
Each heartbeat echoes in the night,
A rhapsody of purest light.

From dawn to dusk, the rhythm flows,
In nature's grace, the spirit grows.
Within the silence, wisdom gleams,
In every breath, a thousand dreams.

Secrets Blooming at Dusk

As daylight fades, the shadows creep,
Soft petals close, the world in sleep.
Whispers rustle in the leaves,
Where secrets bloom as twilight weaves.

Crickets join the evening choir,
While fireflies dance with glowing fire.
Each breath of night, a story spun,
In hushed tones shared, we become one.

The sky, a canvas of deep blue,
Mirrors the dreams that feel so true.
In every corner, treasures hide,
Awaiting those who seek inside.

With every heartbeat, time stands still,
As magic drapes the quiet hill.
The breeze carries forgotten lore,
Of secrets whispered evermore.

So linger here as night unfolds,
Where nature's heart, a tale retolds.
Secrets bloom in the dusky light,
Awakening dreams that take to flight.

Veils of Mist and Magic

In morning's breath, the mist awakes,
A shroud of dreams the daylight makes.
Veils of magic cloak the ground,
In silence, hidden wonders found.

Soft tendrils curl through ancient oaks,
While nature stirs and gently chokes.
The sun peeks through with tender rays,
Igniting hope in brand new ways.

Each drop of dew, a crystal light,
Reflects the dreams of endless night.
With every step, the world unfolds,
Revealing tales that time upholds.

The whispers of the earth coalesce,
In veils of mystery, we are blessed.
A world transformed at every glance,
Inviting hearts to join the dance.

The mist a quilt of soft embrace,
In magic's arms, we find our place.
Where veils of mist and dreams align,
And every moment feels divine.

Elusive Shadows Dancing

In twilight's cloak, the shadows play,
Mysterious forms slip away.
Whispers of secrets in the night,
Glimmers of silver, soft and light.

They weave between the trees so tall,
A dance of dreams beneath it all.
Flickers of spirits, lost and free,
Carrying tales of harmony.

With each step, a story unfolds,
A tapestry of wonders told.
In the stillness, hearts align,
As time slips softly, so divine.

The moonlight drapes in velvet hues,
In the shadows, the world renews.
Whirling like leaves on the breeze,
In silent rhythms, our souls find ease.

The Reverie of Green Enchantment

Amidst the leaves where laughter thrives,
The song of nature gently strives.
Each rustling breeze, a sweet caress,
An emerald world in all its dress.

In tangled vines, the fairies play,
In dappled light, they weave the day.
Colors of spring, so rich and bright,
Dance through the heart, an endless flight.

With every bloom, the magic grows,
In hidden paths, the wonder flows.
A symphony of life anew,
In every shade, a dazzling view.

Beneath the boughs, beneath the sky,
The echoes of the woodlands sigh.
A reverie of green so grand,
In nature's arms, we understand.

Mysteries in the Understory

In depths where sunlight barely glows,
The silent whispers softly close.
A world beneath the towering trees,
Where secrets sway in gentle breeze.

Fungi weave tales upon the ground,
In hidden realms, mysteries abound.
Veins of roots intertwine in grace,
Holding the stories, time won't erase.

Crickets hum in the thickening air,
While shadows linger without a care.
Each rustle tells of life unseen,
In tangled webs where spirits convene.

Beetles glide through the chill of dusk,
In the underbrush, a fragrant musk.
Beyond our view, wonders ignite,
In the bard's embrace, the unseen light.

Harmony of the Starlit Arbor

Beneath the vast celestial dome,
The starlit arbor calls us home.
With twinkling lights, the night unfurls,
In whispered dreams, the magic swirls.

Branches stretch like arms in prayer,
Holding the stories of those who dare.
In shadows deep, the owls take flight,
Guardians of secrets in the night.

Moonbeams catch the dew-kissed grass,
While time stands still, and moments pass.
A symphony from crickets' sound,
In harmony with earth profound.

Amidst the stillness, hearts unite,
In the embrace of soft twilight.
Each star a note in nature's song,
In this starlit haven, we belong.

Evernight's Soft Embrace

In shadows deep where whispers dwell,
The night unfolds its velvet spell.
Stars twinkle in a silent serenade,
While dreams in stillness softly wade.

A cool breeze carries laughter low,
As shadows dance, an ebb and flow.
Moonbeams kiss the silken grass,
In evernight, sweet moments pass.

The owls sing their ancient tune,
Underneath the watchful moon.
Heartbeats blend with nature's song,
Where peace and beauty both belong.

Crickets chirp a lullaby,
As night unfurls its mystic sky.
Wrapped in darkness, love takes flight,
In evernight's soft, warm light.

The Enigma of the Moonlit Thicket

In thickets dense, the shadows play,
Where secrets murmur and spirits sway.
The moon spills silver on the ground,
Embracing all with a mystic sound.

Branches weave a tender shroud,
As night descends, serene and proud.
Each rustle hides a tale untold,
In the thicket's grasp, the night unfolds.

A fleeting glimpse of eyes aglow,
Beneath the boughs where shadows grow.
The enigma dances, whispers rise,
In moonlit thicket 'neath the skies.

Timeless echoes in the air,
A haunting beauty, wild and rare.
In every sigh, a story spins,
The thicket breathes where night begins.

Shimmers on the Elderbough

On elderbough where fairies play,
Soft shimmers lead the night away.
Twinkling lights like glistening dew,
Reveal the magic hidden from view.

In twilight's glow, a gentle breeze,
Murmurs secrets among the trees.
Each petal kissed by twilight's grace,
In nature's arms, we find our place.

The elder blooms with whispers sweet,
As night descends, our hearts may meet.
Beneath its branches, dreams take flight,
In silver beams of soft moonlight.

Elders stand, their wisdom vast,
Guardians of a shadowed past.
With every shimmer, stories weave,
In elder's presence, we believe.

Elven Echoes in the Silent Dark

In silent dark, the echoes call,
Of elves that tread in shadows tall.
Their laughter lingers on the breeze,
A symphony amidst the trees.

Moonlit paths where starlight glows,
Through ancient woods where magic flows.
Each step they take, a whisper rare,
An echo of the dreams they share.

The night unveils a story true,
Of elven joy and sorrows too.
In every shadow, every spark,
Resides the dance of the silent dark.

Timeless tales in soft refrain,
In every sigh, the joy and pain.
Elven spirits weave and roam,
In sacred woods, they find their home.

Echoes of Forgotten Tomes

In dusty halls where whispers swirl,
Ancient pages unfurl,
Secrets held in fragile spines,
Time entangled in the lines.

Faded ink beneath my touch,
Stories linger, mean so much,
Voices lost in ages past,
In these tomes, their shadows cast.

By candlelight, the words awake,
Glimmers of the paths we take,
Words of sorrow, joy, and strife,
Echoes of a borrowed life.

The air is thick with tales untold,
Each breath a memory of gold,
In silence, I hear them call,
The voices rise, the shadows fall.

As I turn each fragile page,
The spirits dwell, not one, but sage,
Together we weave the tales sublime,
Dancing through the arms of time.

The Path of Gossamer Threads

Beneath the sky, a silver line,
Threads of light begin to shine,
Whispers float on gentle breeze,
Nature's secrets, hearts at ease.

In gardens where the daffodils bloom,
Silken strands weave through the gloom,
With every step, a story spins,
In the silence, hope begins.

Through forest paths where shadows play,
Gossamer threads lead the way,
Guiding souls with soft embrace,
Every moment finds its place.

In twilight's grasp, the world will fade,
Yet our spirits dance, unafraid,
Bound by the threads of dreams we share,
In luminous whispers, we declare.

Across the night, they twist and twine,
A tapestry both yours and mine,
On this path, where magic flows,
Together, we will always grow.

Luminescence of the Sylvan Heart

In woodland depths where shadows play,
Light filters through in a gentle sway,
The heart of nature pulses bright,
Guiding lost souls through the night.

Emerald leaves in twinkling waltz,
A sacred dance, no hint of faults,
Whispered secrets in the air,
Underneath the moon's soft glare.

Luminous trails on the forest floor,
Each step reveals what lies in store,
A symphony of rustling tones,
Unity of hearts and stones.

Stars above begin to weave,
A tapestry of light we believe,
In every flicker, hope ignites,
A chorus of forgotten nights.

Embraced by trees as spirits soar,
This sylvan heart forevermore,
Bound to all who seek the glow,
In nature's arms, we come to know.

The Harmonies of Shadow and Light

In twilight's embrace, shadows blend,
A melody plays, seeking to mend,
Dancing figures of dark and bright,
Harmonies born from the night.

Echoes linger where spirits dwell,
In whispered tones, secrets tell,
Between the stars and earth's domain,
A song unites joy and pain.

Every flicker casts a tale,
Where light shines through, shadows pale,
In the weave of dusk and dawn,
A timeless song is gently drawn.

With every breath, we learn to see,
The beauty held in mystery,
Together, they hold hands so tight,
In the harmonies of shadow and light.

Through the veil, we find our way,
In the chiaroscuro ballet,
United by realms, we take our flight,
In the echoes of the night.

Beneath the Boughs of Ancient Dreams

In shades of green where shadows play,
The ancient boughs in whispers sway.
Their stories told in rustling grace,
A tapestry of time's embrace.

Beneath the leaves, a secret song,
Of days gone past, where hearts belong.
Each breeze unveils a memory,
Of tranquil nights and gentle spree.

The roots entwined in earth so deep,
Hold mysteries that nature keeps.
In silence vast, the spirits roam,
In every breath, I feel at home.

The sunlight filters, a golden hue,
Embracing all with warmth anew.
While dreams awaken in twilight's glow,
Beneath the boughs, my soul does grow.

So here I stand, both lost and found,
With every heartbeat, love unbound.
Amidst the branches, life's sweet schemes,
I wander deep in ancient dreams.

Whispers from the Woodland Nook

Amidst the trees, a soft refrain,
The woodland nook calls out my name.
With gentle breeze, the leaves converse,
In hidden tones, the universe.

A step within the emerald shade,
In vibrant whispers, time does fade.
Where shadows dance on forest floors,
And echo laughter through the doors.

The brook nearby sings of the past,
Its bubbling voice a spell is cast.
With every drop, a tale is spun,
Of nature's heart, forever won.

The blossoms nod, with petals bright,
Embracing all in pure delight.
In every corner, magic blooms,
While woodland whispers chase away glooms.

Within this nook, I find my peace,
The world outside, a sweet release.
In nature's arms, my spirit thrives,
In whispers soft, my heart survives.

Serene Secrets of the Eldertree

Beneath the boughs, the elders stand,
With wisdom deep as ancient sand.
Their gnarled limbs bear silent tales,
Of gentle storms and tender gales.

In silent nights, a moonlit view,
The Eldertree speaks truths anew.
As shadows stretch and dreams take flight,
It cradles whispers of the night.

The roots that weave through time and space,
Keep every secret in their grace.
They hold the echoes of the years,
Of laughter, love, and muted tears.

With every rustle of the leaves,
A memory in silence weaves.
The tranquil breaths of days gone by,
In twinkling stars that fill the sky.

So linger long, beneath its shade,
In every glint, a promise made.
The Eldertree, with arms so wide,
Holds all my dreams, where hopes abide.

Beneath the Gossamer Veil of Dusk

As daylight fades, the shadows creep,
The world transforms, the secrets seep.
Beneath the veil of dusky glow,
The night reveals what dreams may show.

The stars emerge, like whispers bright,
In twilight's kiss, they greet the night.
Each twinkle tells of paths unseen,
In silver beams, we drift between.

The moon ascends, a watchful eye,
In silent vigil, it floats high.
Its silver light casts gentle beams,
That weave a world of whispered dreams.

As night unfolds its velvet cloak,
In quietude, the heart awoke.
With every breath, the world stands still,
In dusky hues, I find my will.

So let the evening tides abide,
Within its arms, I take a ride.
Amidst the peace of dusk's embrace,
I find my soul's eternal space.

The Language of Leaves and Light

In whispers soft, the leaves converse,
Their rustling tells of nature's verse.
Beneath the sun, they dance and sway,
A symphony in bright display.

With beams that filter through the trees,
Each moment captured by the breeze.
The golden light on emerald hue,
A timeless tale of old and new.

In twilight's glow, the shadows weave,
A tapestry that few believe.
The silent secrets that they share,
In gentle rustles, everywhere.

The language speaks, though words are few,
In every shade, a meaning true.
A world alive, with stories bright,
In leaves and light, pure sheer delight.

So pause, listen to the sound,
Of life and love that can be found.
For nature's voice, both clear and bright,
Is captured in the leaves of light.

Shimmering Shadows of the Fey Realm

In twilight's cloak, the shadows play,
A dance of sprites, in bright array.
With laughter soft, they weave their tale,
In fleeting forms that swirl and sail.

The glimmering light, a subtle hint,
Of secret paths where dreams imprint.
In whispers low, the breezes sigh,
As starlit eyes watch from nearby.

The forest glows with colors rare,
Each flicker is a spell in air.
The Fey would charm with every glance,
Inviting hearts to join the dance.

A shimmer here, a shadow cast,
An echo of adventures past.
Through thicket dense, the secrets flow,
Where time stands still and magic grows.

So wander forth, if courage bold,
To seek the wonders yet untold.
In Fey's embrace, the world anew,
A tapestry of dreams in view.

The Glistening Pathway to Wonder

A pathway glows with silver light,
Where dreams take shape in whispered night.
Each step leads on to mysteries,
Awakening the heart with ease.

The stars above, they twinkle bright,
A guide for souls in search of flight.
With hope aglow, the journey starts,
A world where magic fills the hearts.

In every turn, a new surprise,
Caught in the warmth of starlit skies.
Adventure waits on every bend,
Where wonders weave, and dreams descend.

The moonbeams dance on branches high,
As nightingale croons lullabies.
The glistening trail, a call to roam,
Leads seekers to their rightful home.

So follow close, with spirit free,
Embrace the charm of mystery.
For every footstep on this path,
Holds treasures rich, and joy to gather.

Celestial Murmurs Through the Arbor

Beneath the trees, where whispers flow,
The cosmos sings, a haunting show.
In every breeze, a starlit thread,
Connecting hearts, where dreams are bred.

The branches sway, a gentle dance,
In moonlit glow, a blessed chance.
With every rustle, secrets shared,
The universe knows, for it has cared.

Celestial murmurs, soft and sweet,
In nature's arms, our souls do meet.
With eyes uplifted to the night,
We find our place in endless light.

The stars above, a map laid bare,
Guiding us through the evening air.
In quiet joy, we walk along,
As heartbeats merge with nature's song.

So linger here, where whispers dwell,
In every story that we tell.
For through the arbor, love's embrace,
Connects the heavens to this place.

The Keeper of Secrets Beneath the Shelter

In shadows deep, the whispers dwell,
Beneath the leaves, they weave their spell.
A guardian stands with history's eyes,
Holding truths where silence lies.

Forgotten tales by starlight's glow,
Creep through the roots, where secrets flow.
The keeper listens, a heart so wise,
Embracing all with gentle sighs.

Beneath the boughs, old dreams reside,
With every breeze, their voices glide.
Time drips like dew from leaf to ground,
In this sacred space, all is found.

Echoes ripple through emerald air,
Stitched in the fabric of earth's own care.
The keeper of lore, beneath the tree,
Guarding stories of what will be.

In twilight's hush, the night unfolds,
As starlight bathes the secrets untold.
In the shelter's arms, they gently rest,
Unraveled dreams in the forest's chest.

Moonlit Pathways of the Ancients

Beneath the moon's soft silver glow,
Ancient stones in silence show.
Whispers of wisdom from ages past,
Guide the wanderer, shadows cast.

Footfalls echo on pathways worn,
With each step, a tale reborn.
Glimmers of magic in the night,
Illuminate the hidden sight.

Through tangled branches, the path weaves,
Amongst the twilight, the spirit believes.
Every turn holds a memory dear,
Calling forth those who wish to hear.

A dance of light through ancient trees,
Rustling leaves in the midnight breeze.
The moonlit way, a sacred call,
Awakening dreams, embracing all.

In the stillness, the heart takes flight,
On ancient pathways in the night.
With every breath, the past ignites,
In moonlit dreams and starry sights.

Horizons of Elven Memories

On the edge of dawn, where starlight fades,
Elven dreams in twilight parades.
Whispers of ages, like soft morning dew,
Kiss the horizon, both timeless and true.

In echoes sweet, the stories flow,
Of ancient woods and rivers slow.
Memories painted in hues divine,
Awake in the heart where they softly shine.

Through glades adorned with the mist of dreams,
Each leaf and petal, a tale that gleams.
Elven laughter in the gentle air,
Dances in light with a magic rare.

As sunbeams stretch across the land,
Time stands still at destiny's hand.
With every breath, the spirits rise,
In horizons where the past lies.

Veils of nature embrace the lore,
Where elven hopes and dreams explore.
In tranquil moments, memories speak,
A language ancient, soft and meek.

Twilight's Embrace on Ferns

In twilight's glow, the ferns entwine,
A whispering soft, with nature's design.
Their emerald arms stretch wide and free,
Cradling the dusk with tender glee.

Twisted shadows dance upon the ground,
Embracing the silence, a soft, sweet sound.
In the stillness, secrets are spun,
Under the gleam of the fading sun.

Dreaming of worlds where time stands still,
Enchanting hearts with a mystic thrill.
Each frond holds whispers of the night,
A lullaby rich in soft twilight.

As stars emerge in the azure dome,
Ferns breathe in rhythm, their tranquil home.
In twilight's embrace, the night descends,
Where magic lingers and silence mends.

A tapestry woven with nature's grace,
In ferns' embrace, we find our place.
With every heartbeat, the earth's soft sigh,
In twilight's arms, we learn to fly.

Secrets of the Enchanted Glade

In the heart where shadows play,
Colors dance and whispers sway,
Mysteries breathe in the night,
Veils of magic, pure and bright.

Ferns and flowers in soft bloom,
Guarding secrets, dispelling gloom,
Footsteps echo on dew-kissed ground,
In this haven, peace is found.

Moonlight trickles through the leaves,
Casting dreams, the heart believes,
Tales of old, in silence told,
In this glade, we're free and bold.

Gentle breeze, a velvet sigh,
Stars above in the velvet sky,
Each glance shared, a tender thread,
In the glade, our spirits fed.

Here we linger, lost in time,
Nature's rhythm, pure and sublime,
Secrets flourished under the shade,
In the light, our fears allayed.

Echoes Beneath the Twilight Canopy

Beneath the branches wide and grand,
Softly whispers the gentle land,
Twilight's glow, a fading light,
Echoes linger, embracing night.

Crickets chirp a lullaby,
As the stars begin to shy,
In the stillness, hearts will race,
Lost in time's warm embrace.

Shadows stretch and softly creep,
In the woods, the secrets sleep,
Every rustle, every sigh,
Holds a tale that never dies.

The twilight hums its ancient song,
Calling for the night so long,
Each moment cherished, held so dear,
In the dark, there's nothing to fear.

In the canopy's gentle shroud,
Life awakens, strong and loud,
With the dawn, the echoes fade,
Yet in our hearts, dreams are laid.

Whispers in the Moonlit Grove

In the grove where shadows blend,
Moonbeams shine, as if to lend,
Silent whispers fill the air,
Secrets spoken, night laid bare.

Each rustle tells a story bold,
Of magic we are yet to hold,
Dreams unfurl like petals white,
In the stillness of the night.

Stars above, a brilliant dance,
Guiding hearts, inviting chance,
In the glow, the world feels new,
In these moments, we break through.

Softly gliding through the haze,
The night unfolds in endless ways,
With every breath, our spirits soar,
In the grove, we're wanting more.

As dawn approaches, shadows wane,
Yet in our souls the whispers reign,
Forever marked by the moonlit gleam,
In this grove, we dare to dream.

The Dance of Light and Shadows

In the dawn where day meets night,
Shadows play in fading light,
A dance begins, both wild and free,
Between the dark and what we see.

Glimmers spark in the slowing breath,
Whispers near the edge of death,
Each moment etched like a song,
In this ballet, we belong.

Hands of dusk, they stretch and sway,
Pulling dreams from night to day,
In this rhythm, we lose our fears,
With every step, we shed our tears.

Flashes bright, like fireflies,
Illuminate the journey's ties,
Embrace the dance, let worries flee,
In the pulse of the mystery.

As twilight fades to evening's shade,
We find our peace in light's cascade,
And though the dance may one day cease,
In our hearts, we find the peace.

Soft Murmurs in Silvan Halls

Whispers drift through ancient trees,
In shadows where the soft wind breathes.
Leaves rustle tales from times of old,
In silvan halls, their secrets told.

Moonlight spills on mossy ground,
A symphony of night resounds.
Crickets chirp their nightly song,
In harmony, we all belong.

Beneath the arching boughs so wide,
The dreams of wanderers softly glide.
With every step, a story grows,
In the twilight, magic flows.

Footfalls fade in gentle grace,
As shadows dance through time and space.
Nature holds her breath in peace,
In silvan halls, our souls release.

Here in stillness, hearts can soar,
In whispered sighs, we seek for more.
Soft murmurs cradle weary minds,
In this embrace, true solace finds.

Twilight Revelations Beneath the Bough

As daylight bids the world goodbye,
The twilight whispers, soft and shy.
Beneath the bough, a dream unfolds,
Where moments linger, tales retold.

Stars awaken in the sky,
Their twinkling eyes begin to pry.
Secrets spill like silver dew,
In gentle hues of purple blue.

Where shadows stretch and echoes play,
The doubts of day are washed away.
With every breath, the night's embrace,
Invites the silence to take place.

Moonbeams dance on forest floor,
Inviting spirits to explore.
Amidst the rustle, hearts ignite,
In twilight's arms, we find our light.

Beneath the bough, we pause and see,
The beauty in tranquility.
A moment's peace, a whispered vow,
In twilight's glow, let's take a bow.

The Unseen Dance of Enchanted Beings

In twilight's veil, the fae convene,
With glimmers bright, their forms unseen.
They twirl beneath the silver glow,
In moonlit realms, where dreams can flow.

With laughter sweet, they weave their art,
In whispers soft that touch the heart.
Each flicker tells of magic's spark,
In the soft realms where dreams embark.

Amongst the flowers, colors blaze,
The air is thick with sweet malaise.
While twigs snap gently under foot,
The dance unfolds, both wild and cute.

With every step, a secret shared,
In shadows deep, we breathe, prepared.
The unseen dance draws us near,
Where wonder reigns and hearts adhere.

With starlit crowns upon their brow,
The beings glide, we watch, and bow.
In nature's arms, they spin and play,
The unseen dance, our hearts' ballet.

The Ethereal Veil of Green

Through emerald leaves, the sunlight streams,
An ethereal veil, where nature dreams.
A tapestry of life unfurls,
In every nook, a story swirls.

The forest breathes with ancient lore,
A sacred space, a twilight door.
Soft shadows murmur, intertwine,
In emerald whispers, hearts align.

Twig and flower, all adorned,
Each petal cradles dreams reborn.
In gentle hues of jade and lime,
The ethereal veil transcends time.

A carpet of moss, so lush and deep,
Invites the soul to pause and leap.
In every rustle, every glance,
The forest holds a timeless dance.

With every breath, the world's embrace,
In nature's heart, we find our place.
The ethereal veil sways and spins,
In quiet peace, true freedom begins.

Starlit Murmurs Among the Roots

Beneath the stars, the whispers flow,
Gentle secrets, soft and low.
Roots entwined in earth's embrace,
Tracing stories in this space.

Moonlight dances on the ground,
Nature's voice, a soothing sound.
In the silence, dreams take flight,
Murmurs echo through the night.

Every rustle, every sigh,
Tales of time, they drift and fly.
Among the roots, the world feels small,
A starlit realm, embracing all.

Footsteps linger, hearts entrust,
Where shadows fall, in soil and dust.
Murmurs weave their tranquil thread,
In the hush where all is said.

Here, within the ancient trees,
Breathe the air that carries ease.
Every night, beneath night's shroud,
Starlit murmurs, safe and loud.

The Veiled Symphony of the Elden Woods

In the shadow of the towering trees,
Whispers float upon the breeze.
Nature's notes, soft and divine,
Craft a symphony, slow and fine.

Leaves converse, a rustling song,
Echoes where they all belong.
Branches sway in rhythmic grace,
Veiled secrets of this place.

Underneath, the roots can dream,
Spirits dance in silver beam.
Elden woods, a timeless stage,
Life unfolds, page after page.

Misty dawn, where shadows play,
Drapes of mystery lead the way.
All around the magic gleams,
In the heart of whispered dreams.

With each footfall, hearts align,
Lost in nature's grand design.
Elden woods, so wise and free,
In your arms, eternity.

Whispers of the Hidden Haven

In a clearing, sunlight spills,
Nature breathes, the silence fills.
Hidden haven, safe and bright,
Whispers woven with the light.

Fern and flower paint the scene,
Softly swaying, lush and green.
Birds converse in playful tunes,
Beneath the gaze of silver moons.

In this place, hearts come to rest,
Among the quiet, feel your best.
Gentle breezes, sweetly sigh,
Secrets spoken, never shy.

Beneath the boughs, the world is still,
Every moment, a gentle thrill.
Nature cradles, embrace so mild,
In hidden haven, every child.

With each whisper, life unfolds,
Stories shared, as time beholds.
Lost in peace, embraced by grace,
In this haven, find your place.

Chronicles of the Whispering Grove

In the grove where silence sleeps,
Ancient stories, buried deep.
Whispers travel with the breeze,
Tales of ages, strong like trees.

Each rustling leaf, a word unheard,
In the stillness, nature stirred.
Chronicles of the past arise,
In the shadows, under skies.

Roots entwined, secrets intertwine,
A world breathes in every line.
Hear the echoes call your name,
In this grove, nothing's the same.

Mossy stones, the wisdom keep,
Guardians in the stillness deep.
Creaking branches share their lore,
Whispering tales of evermore.

Beneath the heavens, hearts unite,
In the grove, all feels just right.
Chronicles flow with every breeze,
In this place, so full of ease.

Breaths of Life in the Wildwood

Deep in the woods where shadows play,
Life dances softly, night and day.
Whispers of leaves in the gentle breeze,
Nature's heartbeat puts the mind at ease.

Beneath the boughs, where stillness dwells,
The story of life in silence tells.
Creatures frolic, the stream flows clear,
In the wildwood's heart, all is sincere.

Roots intertwine in a complex web,
Moss carpets earth with a soothing ebb.
Sunlight filters through emerald crowns,
Each breath a treasure that nature crowns.

Amidst the thicket, tranquility reigns,
Memories echo in the soft refrains.
Time drifts slow, like a soft-spun thread,
In the wildwood's embrace, worries shed.

With every rustle, the wild calls near,
In this sanctuary, there's nothing to fear.
Breaths of life weave a tapestry bright,
In the heart of the wildwood, pure delight.

Song of the Whispering Glades

In glades where secrets and shadows meet,
The winds carry whispers, light and sweet.
A chorus of nature sings in the air,
Each note a promise, a dream laid bare.

Dappled sunlight plays on the forest floor,
As leaves recount tales of ages before.
The brook babbles softly, a soothing sound,
In the glades, serenity is found.

Wildflowers sway in a graceful dance,
Bathed in sunlight, they twirl and prance.
Bees hum a tune, busy in flight,
In this tranquil realm, all feels right.

Tall trees stand sentinel, wise and grand,
Guardians of stories in this enchanted land.
Under their branches, the heartbeats sync,
In harmony, we breathe, pause, and think.

As twilight descends, the birds take flight,
The glades whisper softly, bidding goodnight.
The song of the whispering glades will remain,
A melody echoing in our veins.

Twilight's Embrace of the Ancient

When twilight descends in hues of gold,
The ancient trees wear stories untold.
Beneath their boughs, shadows lengthen wide,
In twilight's embrace, secrets abide.

Starlight begins to sprinkle the sky,
An owl calls out as the day says goodbye.
Time slows its march, in the fading light,
In this sacred hour, the world feels right.

The whispers of night blend with the breeze,
As nature awakens, a symphony frees.
Moonbeams dance softly on leaves that sway,
In twilight's embrace, night steals the day.

Ancient stones, wrapped in mossy grace,
Hold whispers of wisdom in their embrace.
Each moment abundant, each breath a gift,
In twilight's soft glow, our spirits lift.

As stars shine brightly in the tranquil deep,
The ancient wisdom invites us to keep,
In twilight's embrace, we find our way,
Guided by nature, come what may.

The Guardian of Secrets Unseen

In shadows where mysteries quietly dwell,
The guardian stands, with tales to tell.
Watchful and wise, they gaze from the trees,
Guarding the whispers carried by breeze.

Through tangled brambles, and paths overgrown,
Lie secrets safe in places unknown.
The rustle of leaves hides countless dreams,
In worlds woven tight by nature's seams.

Ancient stones hold the weight of time,
With an aura that dances in rhythm and rhyme.
The guardian beckons with a gentle sway,
Inviting the curious to wander and play.

In moonlit glades, where shadows convene,
The stories unfold of what has been seen.
Each flicker of light, each echo of sound,
Holds the pulse of the earth, profound.

With every heartbeat, the secrets reside,
In the depths of the wild, where wonders collide.
The guardian of secrets, both fierce and kind,
Holds the essence of life, in the depths of our mind.

The Lure of Magic in the Mist

In the morning fog, secrets creep,
Where whispers of wonder softly sweep.
The air tingles with each hidden thread,
Inviting the dreamers where shadows tread.

Mystical colors, bright and dim,
Dance on the edges, a tantalizing whim.
A flicker of hope, a glimmer of gold,
In the embrace of the mist, stories unfold.

Invisible hands beckon with care,
Promising treasures that linger in air.
The heart beats faster, the spirit ignites,
Chasing the glimmers that boat on the nights.

From the veil of the moist, a soft spell weaves,
Enticing the souls that the magic believes.
Every turn taken, a path that is new,
Where the lure of enchantment pulls us right through.

So step into wonders that beckon within,
Let the mist wrap around, let the journey begin.
For in every shadow, in every misty gleam,
Lies the pursuit of the wildest dream.

Treetop Serenades at Dusk

As daylight fades, the branches hum,
With melodies soft, the night is begun.
Whispers of breezes, songs of the past,
Where treetops sway, shadows are cast.

Crickets join in with a delicate tune,
Under the watchful eye of the moon.
Branches like fingers sway and embrace,
Nature's sweet serenade in this space.

Rustling leaves tell a story so deep,
Of all that the forest has vowed to keep.
With each gentle sigh, the night comes alive,
In treetop chambers, the joys surely thrive.

Stars peek through, their light softly spills,
A chorus of crickets, the wind gently thrills.
In this twilight realm, where secrets unwind,
A symphony echoes, pure and unconfined.

So close your eyes and let the night sing,
In the heart of the treetops, peace will take wing.
For in serenades whispered through dusk,
Lies a magic that's gentle, tender, and husk.

Elven Lullabies in the Breeze

Softly they sing, the elven refrain,
Carried by breezes, sweet like the rain.
A song of the ancients, gentle and wise,
Echoing through the trees, under starry skies.

With notes like silver, the night air fills,
Stirring the dreams of the daffodil wills.
Each lilting breath from the forest's own heart,
Binding us closer as night will impart.

Moonlit whispers float, serene and calm,
Wrapped in enchantment, pure as a psalm.
The lullabies cradle each soul in embrace,
In this twilight glow, we find our place.

Drawn to the magic, the mystique so rare,
We listen intently, hearts laid bare.
For in every note, a spell is infused,
An elven blessing that leaves us amused.

So linger a while, let the promises soar,
In the breeze of the night, we'll ask for no more.
For in elven lullabies, peace takes its flight,
Guiding us gently into the night.

Silhouettes in the Whispering Wind

Silhouettes dance on the canvas of night,
In the breath of the breeze, shadows take flight.
Figures entwined in a delicate waltz,
Nature's own rhythm, a silent pulse.

Branches stretch high, their fingers hold tight,
Cradling dreams in the soft, fading light.
Each whisper that passes, a secret to share,
In the sway of the wind, all burdens laid bare.

Ghostly reflections, a shimmering sight,
Fleeting like wishes, they slip out of sight.
Yet in every shadow, a story remains,
In the heart of the wind, the magic retains.

So listen closely, and you just might hear,
The echoes of laughter, the sighs of a sphere.
For silhouettes linger, though daylight is done,
In the whispering wind, our souls become one.

To dance in the dusk with each fleeting form,
Embracing the night as the shadows transform.
In every gentle breeze, we find a friend,
In silhouettes lost, where the whispers tend.

When the Stars Hold Their Breath

In velvet night, the stars align,
A stillness wraps the world in time.
Whispers in the cosmic glow,
Secrets that the heavens know.

The moonlight dances on the sea,
Reflecting dreams that long to be.
Each twinkle speaks of tales untold,
Of lovers lost and knights so bold.

A quiet peace enfolds the land,
As shadows stretch and softly stand.
The air is thick with fate's design,
When stars hold breath, all is divine.

In that moment, hearts collide,
Underneath the glowing tide.
Time distorts, and souls take flight,
In the stillness of the night.

So let us pause, and let us pause,
Embrace the night without a cause.
For when the stars, in silence, sway,
The magic lives in every ray.

Beneath the Eldertree's Embrace

Under branches thick and wise,
Where sunlight struggles, shy and high.
The whispers of the ancients bloom,
In the Eldertree's shaded room.

Each knot and gnarled twist tells tales,
Of fleeting winds and joyous gales.
Roots deep in stories rich and old,
Cradle dreams that hearts have told.

Dappled light, a golden hue,
Wraps secrets where the shadows grew.
A nest of memories is laid,
In the silence, spirits fade.

Children play in spirit's dance,
Amongst the leaves, a timeless trance.
The tug of time gently recedes,
Beneath the tree that ever feeds.

So linger here, where love abides,
In the embrace where hope resides.
With every breath, feel time erase,
All sorrows, here, beneath this space.

Hushed Chants of the Woodland Spirits

In the glen where shadows sleep,
Whispers rise from secrets deep.
Mossy stones and trunks so bare,
Hold the echoes of the air.

Faint melodies drift on the breeze,
A song of old, the heart will please.
Spirits gather, soft and light,
In the hush of fading night.

Leaves tremble with a gentle sigh,
Beneath the stars that dot the sky.
Ancient hymns, a sacred trust,
As voices blend with earth and dust.

Through tangled brambles, soft and shy,
Silent prayers float and fly.
Each note a droplet, pure and clear,
Calling all who wish to hear.

So venture forth where shadows dance,
Join the spirits in their trance.
For in the woods, where echoes play,
Hushed chants guide the light of day.

Serenade of the Hidden Realm

In the twilight's soft embrace,
Mysteries weave, a hidden trace.
Celestial paths, where dreams reside,
In the realm where fates confide.

Glimmers float through silent air,
Sparking joy beyond compare.
With every step, enchantments bloom,
In shadows deep, dispelling gloom.

Moments linger in the haze,
Caught in time's ethereal maze.
Each whisper carries tales of old,
Of love, of loss, of lives retold.

Faint laughter echoes, sweet and light,
In the dimming of the fading light.
A serenade, both soft and grand,
Guiding hearts to understand.

So let us wander, hand in hand,
Through the magic of this land.
For in the hidden, we are free,
In the serenade's soft decree.

Tread Lightly on Fern-Laden Paths

In shadows deep where ferns unfurl,
Soft whispers greet as breezes swirl.
Ancient roots hold secrets tight,
Inviting steps to dance in light.

With every step, the ground will sigh,
As nature's pulse beats low and high.
A symphony of leaves in play,
Guides wanderers along the way.

Emerald carpets, rich and bright,
A world where day meets gentle night.
The forest breathes, a timeless art,
Inviting wanderers to pause their heart.

Beneath the boughs, life intertwines,
With every flicker, the magic shines.
Footfalls soft as dreams take wing,
In fern-laden paths, the spirits sing.

So tread with care, embrace the calm,
The forest wraps you in its balm.
For every trail, a story spun,
In nature's arms, we are all one.

The Moonlit Caress of Hidden Realms

Beneath the moon's soft silver gleam,
Whispers drift like a lucid dream.
Hidden realms where shadows weep,
Awake in night's most silken deep.

Stars weave tales of yesteryears,
Embracing hearts while calming fears.
The night unveils a sacred song,
Guiding souls who have wandered long.

In the embrace of gentle night,
Where every spark ignites the light.
Mysteries stir under lunar eyes,
As echoes of the past arise.

The air thick with the scent of pine,
As secrets linger, intertwine.
Through every shadow, hope will swell,
In moonlit realms where spirits dwell.

So dance beneath the starry dome,
Lost in magic, forever roam.
For in each flicker of twilight's breath,
Lie hidden dreams, untouched by death.

Etherial Tales of the Green Grove

In whispers low, the groves bestow,
Tales of life in verdant flow.
Mossy carpets greet the feet,
Where time and nature gently meet.

Dancing leaves in summer's warm,
Invite each spirit to transform.
The sunlight filters through the trees,
With laughter carried on the breeze.

Every rustle holds a lore,
Each creature's path reveals a door.
To realms where ancient echoes play,
In green groves, hearts drift away.

Through briar and bloom, the stories weave,
Promises held in the air we breathe.
In twilight's hush, the magic grows,
In every petal, a secret flows.

So venture forth where spirits thrive,
In the tapestry of life, we strive.
For every tale, a journey shared,
In the green grove, all hearts are bared.

Notes from the Heart of the Moss

Upon the floor where mosses lay,
Nature hums in a soft ballet.
Each cushion whispers tales of old,
In shades of green and whispers bold.

The heart of moss, a gentle beat,
Cradles life in a soft retreat.
Where time stands still, the breezes talk,
In harmony, the shadows walk.

Layered dreams, a textured story,
In every nook, a hint of glory.
The world unveiled, a sacred art,
As nature paints upon our heart.

Within the depths of emerald hue,
A symphony of life rings true.
As creatures pause and linger near,
In mossy realms, all things are clear.

So listen close to the earth's sighs,
In the heart of moss, beauty lies.
For in its embrace, peace will dwell,
In whispered notes, the world will swell.

Whispers of Time in Elven Glades

In the heart of the wood, whispers dwell,
Ancient secrets of time they tell.
Gentle breezes carry the lore,
Echoes of legends, forevermore.

Moonlight dances on silken leaves,
Casting shadows where magic weaves.
Elven laughter fills the night,
In glades aglow with a soft, pale light.

Amidst the trees, dreams gently stir,
A world of wonder begins to blur.
Each step forward, a tale unfolds,
In whispers of time, the forestholds.

Beneath the stars, destinies align,
Every heartbeat sings, pure and divine.
Nature's melody, tender and clear,
Guides the lost, drawing them near.

So linger in silence, let your thoughts flow,
In elven glades where echoes grow.
For every moment is a timeless dance,
A whispering promise, a second chance.

Luminous Dreams Under the Stars

Beneath the vast canvas, the starlight glows,
A tapestry woven by fate's soft prose.
Luminous dreams take flight in the night,
Guided by constellations, a radiant sight.

Whispers of hope in the cosmic sea,
Every twinkle, a wish, wild and free.
The universe beckons with each kind flare,
Inviting the dreamer to breathe in the air.

Calm is the night, with stories untold,
In silvery beams, the future unfolds.
With each gentle breeze, doubts cast away,
The heart finds its rhythm, in night's sweet sway.

The moon wears a crown of shimmering light,
A guardian's gaze on the canvas of night.
In moments of stillness, the soul takes flight,
Luminous dreams, woven in pure delight.

Through whispers of stardust, we navigate time,
With the heart as our compass, we rise, we climb.
In the depths of the cosmos, we find our peace,
A dance of the galaxies, a gentle release.

Flickering Fantasies Through the Boughs

In the thick of the woods, fantasies flicker,
Through branches and boughs, they weave and snicker.
Soft songs of the forest lift spirits high,
Like whispers of wind that twirl and fly.

Each fluttering leaf holds a secret so dear,
Fables of wonder, a world without fear.
Dancing shadows paint stories in play,
In the flicker of dreams, we drift away.

The ethereal glow from the faraway streams,
Encourages hearts to awaken their dreams.
With every soft rustle, the wild calls true,
Flickering fantasies, inviting anew.

Beneath the wide sky, an infinite call,
Each heartbeat echoes, a siren's enthrall.
In the grand tapestry woven of green,
Flickering lights reveal what's unseen.

So wander the paths where the magic is found,
Delve into dreams where no limits surround.
For in the embrace of the forest so vast,
Flickering fantasies lead us at last.

Heartbeats Beneath the Canopy

In the hush of the woods, heartbeats align,
Beneath a green canopy, where shadows entwine.
Rustling leaves whisper tales of the past,
In nature's embrace, we find peace at last.

Each pulse is a promise, a vibrant note,
The song of the forest in unison wrote.
With each gentle heartbeat, we learn to believe,
In love and in friendship, and what we can achieve.

Through tangled vines, our spirits ignite,
In the glow of the sun, our fears take flight.
Awake in the moment, alive in the now,
Heartbeats beneath trees, they teach us just how.

Interwoven paths connect every being,
A symphony played in the dance of the freeing.
In the quiet of nature, our souls meet their call,
Heartbeats united, together we stand tall.

So venture beneath where the wild things grow,
Listen to heartbeats, let their rhythm flow.
In the tapestry woven, we find our place,
Beneath the green canopy, bound by grace.

The Call of Celestial Roots

In whispers carried by the night,
Stars call forth their ancient light.
Their roots entwined in cosmic dance,
Awakening our souls' expanse.

Beneath a canopy of dreams,
The universe softly gleams.
Each twinkle holds a secret true,
A memory born within the blue.

From depths of silence, shadows rise,
Guiding hearts with emerald skies.
In every pulse, the cosmos hums,
As nature's heartbeat gently thrums.

Invoke the spirits, join the song,
Where we, the dreamers, all belong.
Amidst the roots that intertwine,
The call of home, the spark divine.

Step forth into the midnight air,
Feel the magic woven there.
With open hearts, let visions flow,
To where the seeds of stardust grow.

Mystical Secrets in the Starlight

Upon the canvas of the night,
Mystical secrets come to light.
Each star a keeper of the past,
Whispers of time forever cast.

In the vastness, echoes play,
Cosmic dances on display.
A spellbound world of dreams takes flight,
Guided by the starlit sight.

With open arms, we seek and find,
Treasures hidden, intertwined.
Glimmers of wisdom, soft and clear,
The universe draws us near.

Beneath the veil of endless night,
Our spirits soar, taking flight.
Boundless wonder in each gaze,
Lost in the starlit maze.

As comets trace their fiery trails,
We weave our tales upon the sails.
Mystical secrets in our hands,
Echo of dreams in foreign lands.

Beneath the Bow of Eternity

Beneath the bow of timeless grace,
The universe reveals its face.
In shadows deep, in colors bright,
We find our place in endless night.

With every heartbeat, echoes call,
The threads of fate, they intertwine all.
In soft embrace of starlit skies,
The hopes of ages never die.

A gentle breeze stirs the trees,
Whispers through branches carry ease.
As we float on dreams that soar,
Beneath the bow, our spirits roar.

From ancient roots, the cosmos blooms,
In every heart, the starlight looms.
With open eyes, we seek and see,
The boundless love of mystery.

Embrace the night, let worries fade,
Under the bow, no debts are paid.
In eternity's tender thrall,
We find our truth, we heed the call.

Dreams Woven in the Canopy

In slumber's hold, the world dissolves,
As whispers spin, our fate evolves.
Dreams woven softly, piece by piece,
Within the canopy, find our peace.

With every sigh, a story we share,
Floating on the breath of air.
Colors swirl in silent streams,
Awakening the heart of dreams.

Among the shadows, visions glide,
In the depths of night, we confide.
The stars entwine with hopes and fears,
Embracing all through countless years.

Beneath the branches, our spirits twirl,
As night unfurls its cosmic pearl.
In sacred silence, we unite,
Lost in the beauty of the night.

So linger here, where wishes grow,
In the canopy, let love flow.
Together, we will drift and roam,
In dreams woven, we find our home.

The Unseen Chorus of the Forest

Whispers weave through ancient trees,
A melody on the gentle breeze.
Birds join in with ecstatic flight,
Nature sings beneath the light.

Leaves clap softly, their rhythm divine,
As sunbeams dance on vines that entwine.
Mossy carpets, a plush embrace,
Guide the wanderer through time and space.

Roots entangle in sacred ground,
In this chorus, life is found.
From the soil, a symphony grows,
Echoes of secrets that the forest knows.

Crisp air holds an electric tune,
Beneath the gaze of the silver moon.
Every rustle, a note in the song,
Calling the lost, where they belong.

In the stillness, the heart will hear,
The unseen chorus, ever near.
Nature's voice, tender and true,
A hymn for me, a hymn for you.

Dreams Weaved in Silver Threads

In the twilight, dreams take flight,
Weaved in silver, soft and light.
Whispers of hopes, gentle and clear,
Guide the wanderers, drawing near.

Stars twinkle with secrets untold,
Threads of silver, shiny and bold.
Each wish carries a spark of fate,
In the loom of night, we create.

Minds like rivers, flowing fast,
With dreams that stitch the present and past.
In the silence, visions bloom,
Encased in the threads that lighten the gloom.

When dawn rises, dreams take form,
Bathed in sunlight, they quietly warm.
Yet beneath that morning thread,
Lies the silver of thoughts unsaid.

Hold them close, these precious strands,
Cautious journeys on soft sands.
Every dream a spark, a glow,
In silver threads, our futures flow.

Phantoms Dancing through Mossy Glades

In shadows deep, the phantoms play,
Through mossy glades where night turns gray.
They swirl in silence, soft and light,
Echoes of laughter in the moonlit night.

Whispers roam on the misty breeze,
The forest holds its secrets with ease.
Each footfall stirs the dense, cool ground,
In their dance, enchantment is found.

Glimmers flicker, soft and surreal,
Phantoms waltz, an ethereal reel.
Among the ferns, they weave their art,
Holding the magic of every heart.

Time stands still in this sacred space,
As shadows twirl in an endless race.
Each breath a promise, every glance,
Within the dark, we find our chance.

Then dawn will break, the phantoms hide,
Yet in our dreams, they will abide.
For in the glades where memories lay,
Their dance lingers on, come what may.

Celestial Hues of Nature's Veil

When dawn awakens with soft embrace,
Nature dons her stunning lace.
Celestial hues adorn the skies,
As sunlight dances, the darkness dies.

Fields aglow with golden light,
Each petal shines, a wondrous sight.
Butterflies flit as the colors blend,
In this tapestry, hearts transcend.

Mountains rise with a majesty bold,
In crimson and azure, stories unfold.
Rivers glisten like mirrors wide,
Reflecting the beauty nature cannot hide.

Evening whispers of indigo dreams,
In twilight's grasp, the world redeems.
Stars peek out, a velvety brush,
Painting the sky in a tranquil hush.

Nature's veil, a touch of grace,
Holds every color, every space.
In her embrace, we find our way,
Chasing the hues of each new day.

9 781805 598503